Richard Walker

image + myth

This book is dedicated to the memory of my parents, Kathleen and Ken

TREASURE BOOK 1963 DRAWING

Richard Walker
image + myth

Paul Holberton publishing, London

ISBN I 903470 24 2

British Library Cataloging in
Publication Data
A catalogue record for this book is
available from the British Library

Produced by
Paul Holberton publishing
37 Snowsfields, London SE1 3SU
www.paul-holberton.net

Designed by Peter Campbell

Printed by Graphic Studio,
Verona, Italy

UNLESS OTHERWISE STATED, WORKS ARE
MIXED MEDIA ON PAPER, CANVAS OR
WOOD. IN THIS CASE, MIXED MEDIA
MEANS A CHANGING COMBINATION OF
MATERIALS SUCH AS ACRYLIC, WATER-
COLOUR, PASTEL, PENCIL, COLLAGE,
SPRAY PAINT AND TRANSFER PRINTING.
OVER THE YEARS, THESE TECHNIQUES
HAVE EVOLVED, BEEN DEVELOPED AND
SIMPLIFIED.

COVER: FOGGY NOTION 2001 PAPER
21 X 25 CM (DETAIL)

Thank you ...
to Peter Parker, my oldest friend, for doing the interview,
to Simon Doonan, for his reminiscences of the Punk years;
to Chris Rogers, for his review of the murals at Axis
Restaurant; to Jill and John Hutchings, for all their support
and to Gordon Marsden, for always being there.

Contributors:
Simon Doonan is the creative director of Barney's, New York,
an author, a fashion commentator and a columnist for *The
New York Observer*.

Peter Parker is the author of *The Old Lie* (1987) and biographies
of J.R. Ackerley (1989) and Christopher Isherwood (2004). He
is an editor of the Oxford Dictionary of National Biography
and also writes about books and gardening for a wide variety
of publications.

Chris Rogers is an architectural researcher and writer. He
creates and leads tours for the Twentieth Century Society and
writes for its newsletter. He contributed to *Portrait of a Practice:
Pearson Centenary at the Architectural Association* in 2004.

A note about the quotations:

*I have credited all the quotations from writers, artists and musicians,
where possible, and have made every effort to obtain permission from
all those concerned. If however I have infringed any copyrights,
I apologise, and will correct this in any future printings of this book.*

RW

I cannot paint but I love you
Jane Morris to Dante Gabriel Rossetti

1. MODERN JAZZ 1998 PAPER 100 X 70CM (DETAIL)

When to the sessions of sweet silent thought
I summon up remembrance of things past ...

Shakespeare, *Sonnets*, XXX

Where did it all come from? A glimpse of England. The late 1950s. Another planet. After the war, after the rain: My mother in a summer dress on a lawn of dappled sunlight. Me, pudding-bowl hair and stripey socks. Wax crayons and rolls of plain lining paper. Old school exercise books. Making do. Always drawing – on the grass, on the carpet, behind the sofa, on the bed. Plans and designs, maps and diagrams. Building houses from cardboard boxes and blankets ... a strange little world. Marmite sandwiches and a glass of milk.

The 1960s – black and white into colour. Kodachrome slides. A dog in orbit, my father in lightweight suits. Made in America. A new age dawning ....

Jump cut: a cinema in my eyes and a record player in my head. Leafy Surrey. Happy days of scented honeysuckle and longing. 1967 – boarding school in Dorset. A Victorian pile. A pastoral setting with encroaching suburbia. Through a Gothic window, in early autumn, a dark study bedroom. Pre-Raphaelite posters, psychedelic music, a fashionable decadence. Shades of *If* .... A certain sensibility. A little mystery. The windy park in *Blow-Up*. A teenager in love. A poetic young man entering the age of inexperience ... writing poems, illustrating dreams.

Growing up, leaving school – the tower blocks and rainy streets of South London. 1973 – academic echoes in the Arts and Crafts studios of Camberwell. The shock of the old. Entering an austere life of lettering and printing presses. Hot metal and cold corridors. A restless nature, a time for change. Breathing in silkscreen inks and getting high. Kindred spirits. Prints, editions, multiples.

1. RW, SKETCH BY MOTHER 1950s   2. MINSKY'S GALLERY 1985   3. CURIOUS 1996 CANVAS 25 X 20 CM

1976 – my world catches fire. Romantic ideals meet trash
culture. Punky reggae party. Fashionable Chelsea. A smashing
time. Out on the town. Putting it about. Minsky's Gallery 1978
– one-man show business. Cocktails and laughter. Art games
– Tom Phillips's *A Humument*. General Idea's *Reconstructing
Futures*. Eno's *Oblique Strategies*. Peter Greenaway's *The Falls*.
Andrew Logan's *Alternative Miss World*. Heroes and icons –
Lindsay Kemp, Kenneth Anger, Derek Jarman ....
Another world lost.

Onwards and ever upwards: New York, 1978 – a template,
a muse, an attitude. The big picture. 'Here in the city of
shows ....' Steam rising from under the streets. Cultures/
sub-cultures. Sketchbooks as diaries. Postcards as reference.
Photo-booth babies. Be-my-Xerox. Life after Rauschenberg.
The blink of the camera. The zoom of the Super 8. The silver
ghost of Warhol riding on a sea of white noise. Laurie
Anderson talking very slowly. Philip Glass playing very fast.
Brian Eno embracing silence.

Crossing the divide: upscale onto canvas. An international
language. The 1980s. The power of the city – from the centre
to the edges and back. Impossible perspective and vertigo.
Dark travels – in Berlin by the wall. Fear and loathing in
Tangier. The world at one ... at once. On into landscape: free
brushstrokes floated over grids. Stretched horizons,
vanishing points. Twelve hours of sunset across Death Valley.
Zabriskie Point – an exploding dreamhome, fridges and TV
sets floating through space. Slow motion tracking. Highway
blues and desert songs. Blocks of colour, layers of collage.
Paint: scraped, spattered, scratched.

1. SELF-PORTRAIT 1985 DRAWING   2. & 3. SELF PORTRAITS 1997 LIGHT PROJECTION

1

2

3

The 1990s. The elements of architecture: edges, blurs, shadows, relief. Pilgrimages – a visit to Corbusier's Paris. A trip in a rusty old car to Arizona to see Frank Lloyd Wright's 'Taliesin West'. Ancient times and modern movements – white shapes in big landscapes under blue skies. Concrete, steel and glass. Corporate heaven.Young lawyers, sharp suits. The artist as businessman. Pushing ideas and pumping irony: onto walls, into restaurants, onto glass, into store windows.

A new century arrives. Promises and sadness. New tools, new toys and a new skin. The superimposition of the past, present and future. Security, anxiety, celebrity .... A new world order. Happy/sad. Punk/pastoral: stray images from exotic places, half-remembered, half-forgotten. Visions of Utopia, glimpses of Arcadia, clips of cinema, echoes of music. The loneliness of the long-distance artist. Days of low light and Radio 4. Cycling to my studio: the sea and the sky. Simple things. My life as one long love affair with the photocopier. The landscape ahead is full of ghosts and dreams. History as the new future. A child plays alone. The TV is turned down.

Back to the wall. Back to the beginning. Back to work.

Richard Walker, June 2004

The moment you cheat for the sake of beauty, you know you're an artist

David Hockney

1. INKY HEAVEN 1994 MONOPRINT 100 X 70 CM   2. INSTINCTIVE PINK 1994 MONOPRINT 100 X 70 CM   3. UNEASY LIVING EXHIBITION CARD THUMB GALLERY 1981   4. A.M WORLD 1977 SCREENPRINT 24 X 24 CM

Yorkshire 1960 – some of my earliest drawings were of plumbing. When I was aged about six, the pipes on both the inside and the outside of buildings fascinated me. Whenever we visited friends or relations, or stayed in a hotel on holiday, I was usually to be found in the bathroom, lying on the floor with my drawing book. This interest moved on into architecture, then into designing both aircraft and, curiously ... airships. I think I even dreamt up an ocean liner.

Unsurprisingly, I never wanted to be a footballer.

It takes ten years to learn how to draw, and another ten to learn how to draw like a child

Pablo Picasso

My art teacher at school was Robin Noscoe, a twentieth-century Renaissance man and a true inspiration. Everybody used to call him 'Boss' partly because he didn't like to be seen as a schoolmaster, and partly as a mark of respect. Several years before me, the young Derek Jarman had fallen under Robin's spell and later considered him to be a major influence on his own life and work. My generation used to take refuge from the harsh realities of boarding school in the 'Art Shack' – one of the many buildings he designed and built himself, with help from us, his pupils. After leaving school, I kept up with Robin, visiting him and his family in his quirky, modernist home, which he built in an old orchard in Dorset. We often used to draw and paint together and went on jaunts to places like Dublin and Paris. Sadly, he died in 2002, and his house came down a year later.

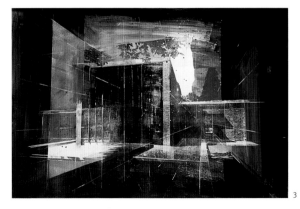

1. ROBIN NOSCOE (THE 'OLD ART SHACK' CANFORD) 1968 DRAWING (DETAIL)   2. ROBIN NOSCOE, PARIS 1990 PHOTOGRAPH   3. STATE OF THE ART (THE 'NEW ART SHACK' CANFORD) 2000 PAPER 70 X 100CM

Autumn 1973 – My first day
at Camberwell was spent in a
lofty Victorian studio, sitting
at a school desk learning
about the spaces between
lettering. The teacher had
a white beard and wore a
smock. By the evening, I was
wondering whether I had
come to the right place ....

1

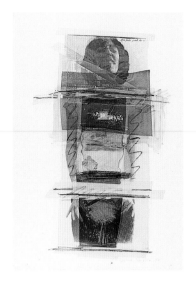

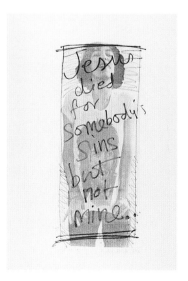

Camberwell 1975 – Patti Smith came along at exactly the right time. There was something in the air during that period – rebellion, unrest and the seeds of an pop-art/punk-rock crossover. Patti was an ideal muse. Artist, icon, poet, musician and bohemian … she even lived in New York. Her image and influence gave me the freedom and confidence to go my own way and develop my early print/collage/text experiments.

I finally got to meet her in 2003.

Born to be. Born to be me.
Just the right dark glasses.
The power of the image.
Treat the cornea like a jewel.
Sapphire seurat dot.
Pull vision in. Inverted flashlight

Patti Smith, from *Balance* 1974

2

1. CAMBERWELL 1973 WATERCOLOUR 40 X 30 CM   2. CULT FIGURE 1– 6 (PATTI SMITH) 1976 SCREENPRINTS EACH 70 X 48 CM

Smashing Time.

1

1977 was insane. We screamed and yodeled and drank too much and shagged as often as possible and got dressed up in hot-pink and rubber fetish-wear and Pacamacs and plaid bondage outfits.

Brenda's Silver Jubilee, whether celebrated with painful sincerity or jeering irony, added to the cacophony. And there was a great dyke club called Louise's which became a punk club and a snooty club called Zanzibar. We called it Zanzibore and boycotted it (i.e. we weren't allowed in) in favor of a place down the street called The Blitz which became a huge fashion-punk hang-out where Biddie and Eve did their cabaret act. Every weekend the place was jammed with young reprobates like Richard, all singing "Blue, blue 'lectric blue, that's the color of my room" at the top of their lungs. There was an infantile mayhem in the air.

1977 was the year that Richard screen-printed an image of a man and woman screaming and called it "Smashing Time". This artwork was created from an enlarged booth photo portrait of Richard and a girl called Debbie who screamed so much she was given the nick-name Sweep after Sooty's female companion.

Debbie was one of those fashion visionaries that other girls wanted to look like and/or kill. She had bleached hair and Baby Jane make-up and wore fishnets and stilettos and pink synthetic chiffon headscarves instead of clothes. Debbie was an important muse slash alter-ego for Richard. He even dressed as Debbie on Halloween that year.

Cross-dressing and dressing up were part of the Blitz scene. In 1977, Richard expressed himself via an explosive collection of female alter-egos. Though he was and is quite proper and well-brought up, his female incarnations were downwardly mobile strident harridans who lived lives of fragile glamour.

There was Concepta Murphy, a belligerent blonde who lived with her mother Beryl (writer Peter Parker) in Brixton. Beryl and Concepta's impromptu performance art included the staging of guerrilla fashion shows at jumble sales followed by amateur ballroom dancing evenings with middle-aged Pakistani men at Kensington Town Hall. Richard also enjoyed an improbably strong visceral identification with actress Lynn Redgrave and was given to impersonating her in Georgy Girl mode.

His favorite character, however, was Yvonne, the thick-thighed ambitious girl from Bradford, played with astounding verve by Redgrave in the movie Smashing Time, hence his appropriation of the title for above mentioned work.

Though Richard's work matured and shed its overlay of female attention-seeking hysteria, there is nothing superficial about his early prints. Looking back at 1977 and the chaotic punky explosive quality of Smashing Time, it is clear that Richard not only contributed to the fracas of Punk but captured its essence in his art.

Simon Doonan

2

1. SMASHING TIME 1977 SCREENPRINT 70 X 48 CM   2. SMASHING TIME 1977 SKETCHBOOK

Glamour, mayhem and gossip ...

The exhibition of silkscreen prints and mixed media drawings under the title 'One-Man Show Business' (Minsky's Gallery, London) merits examination from two almost contrary positions. Technically both prints, such as 'Camberwell Emmanuelle', 'Blank Generation' (two camera eyes imposed on a porn text) and 'Cosmetic Job' (a 1970s memento mori), and drawings (portraits of models and their friends) are superb, which is no more than one would expect of a young artist whose academic progress was Kingston, Camberwell (BA) and Chelsea (MA). The subject matter, however, is of that tight corner where glamour, mayhem and gossip overlap; and, therefore, not worth the expertise lavished upon it. When he's outgrown Warhol, Hamilton and others of that canaille, and addresses his talents to some subject of value, I think we can expect master work from Richard Walker.

Max Wykes-Joyce, Arts Review, March 1978

Things may come and things may go,
but the art school dance goes on forever

Pete Brown and Piblokto! 1970

1. KISS LAMINATED ENTERTAINS... 1976 SKETCHBOOK   2. BLANK GENERATION 1976 SCREENPRINT 48 X 70 CM   3. COSMETIC JOB 1977 SCREENPRINT 70 X 48 CM

I had a little letter full of paper
inky scratches everywhere
always looking, looking for a paradise island
help me find it everywhere

Robin Williamson, from *Ducks on a Pond* 1968

1. MOONBOYS 1986 PAPER 76 X 56 CM 2. A TALKING PICTURE 1984 SKETCHBOOK

I have used figures in my work since the early days, but they are often incidental, and usually anonymous shapes in some vast picture plane. As a student, I collaged heads and torsos from lonely hearts columns in magazines, then, in the 1980s, I juxtaposed fragments of swimmers and athletes with palm trees and yuccas to celebrate the LA Olympic Games. Later on, I grouped figures in city streets, indicating architectural scale and perspective, but also suggesting alienation and claustrophobia.

Over the years, I've continued to paint angels, gods, devils, ghosts, masks, beasts, lost souls and, more obliquely – self portraits.

1. ACTING HEADS 1982 SKETCHBOOK   2.EGYPTIAN HEADS 1982 SKETCHBOOK

*Remember that the most beautiful things
in the world are the most useless; peacocks
and lilies, for example*

John Ruskin

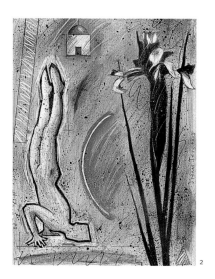

1. ROMANTIC NOTION 1985 PAPER 76 X 56 CM   2. DREAM TERRITORY 1985 PAPER 76 X 56 CM   3. LANGUE D'AMOUR 1985 SKETCHBOOK

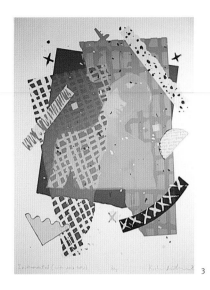

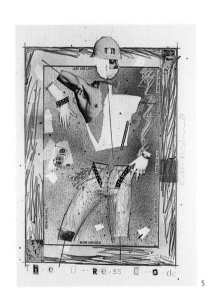

Here's a man who lives a life of danger.
Everywhere he goes, he stays – a stranger

Laurie Anderson, from *Big Science* 1982

1. DECEPTIVE NATURE 1982 SCREENPRINT 70 X 48 CM   2. FALLING IDOL 1982 SCREENPRINT 70 X 48 CM   3. INSTRUMENTAL (WITH VOICE OVER) 1982 SCREENPRINT 70 X 48 CM

4. JAVELIN (LOS ANGELES OLYMPICS) 1984 DRAWING 76 X 56 CM   5. THE DRESS CODE 1981 PAPER 56 X 38 CM   6. HENRY THE HORSE 1979 SCREENPRINT 70 X 48CM

Swimmers
half submerged,
partly revealed –
random dots across
a broken surface.
Bathers by Walter Sickert
and Richard Hamilton.
Children's voices.
Ripples of innocence.
Calm disturbed
by personal challenge –
a crashing wave on
the edge of the world.

A drop in the ocean.

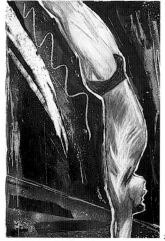

1. EXTENDING CITY LIMITS 1981 PAPER 56 X 38 CM   2. NIGHT FLIGHT 1986 PAPER 76 X 56 CM   3. SWIMMERS 2004 PHOTOGRAPHS   4. MESOPOTAMIA 1998 PAPER 100 X 70 CM (DETAIL)

Living on the Front Line Brixton, South London 1976 – I lived here with my school friend, Peter Parker, when I was an art student. We rented an upstairs flat off Railton Road. Think *Goodbye to Berlin*. Think Warhol's Factory. Post-pop, pre-punk, post-hippy, pre-riots. It looked and felt like parts of New York City ... a walk on the wild side which I was yet to take.

New York City, Summer 1978 – I was one of Freddie Laker's children arriving in the New World. The first generation of wide-eyed explorers to take advantage of the cheap fares on jumbo jets. Nowadays this is commonplace, but at that time the USA was still uncharted territory to most Europeans.

Even as late as the 1970s, it was still a mythical country, only glimpsed through television, popular music and the movies. I was anticipating the sense of freedom, the escape from an English education, and the feeling of endless space. New York had all these, and the space was vertical.

The buidings here were how I used to draw them when I was six years of age; a tangle of drainpipes, lethal wiring, fire escapes and television aerials. I stayed in something similar, that hot and humid summer – a loft on Grand Street, way downtown. Half the space was filled with sound sculptures made of steel and glass. There was no privacy and only one cool fan.The view from the rear was mysterious and shadowy – a sunless corridor of backyards. There were also smells – gasoline, pretzels, laundromats ... and noise, all night noise ... of distant sirens and thundering trucks.

The images that I was to create when I returned home had already been formed in my childhood imagination. I knew this place. It was all so familiar.

1. RW, MAYALL RD BRIXTON 1975   2. BABEL ON 5TH AVENUE 1978 SCREENPRINT 70 X 48 CM   3. MADLY MANHATTAN 1979 SCREENPRINT 48 X 70 CM

In 1988 I painted a picture of Times Square, New York, which was exhibited in Los Angeles and bought by the producer of the TV show *Cagney and Lacey*. I used the title *Civilisation* in an ironic way, thinking it looked more like the end of civilisation, rather than a celebration of it. This image went on to be published as a poster (along with several others, including *Power of the City*). It proved to be a big seller, and hangs on many a student's wall, especially in Germany. For a while, it made me feel like a pop star, but that's another story ....

1. SUBTERRANEANS 1990 PAPER 142 X 102 CM   2. CIVILISATION 1988 PAPER 102 X 84 CM

1. POWER OF THE CITY 1989 PAPER 102 X 142 CM   2. MODERNISTS 1997 PAPER 152 X 122 CM   3. EL DORADO 1990 PAPER 152 X 114 CM   4. ELECTRICITY 1999 CANVAS 153 X 117CM

1. PRIMITIVE FUTURES 1990 PAPER 142 X 102 CM   2. NOCTUNAL 1999 PAPER 74 X 59 CM   3. DEEP STREET DIVING 1996 PAPER 152 X 122 CM   4. ELEGY 2001 CANVAS 213 X 152CM

*Life is oh so sweet above 14th Street
let's go and see how the other half lives*

Loudon Wainwright III, from *Uptown* 1971

1. BROADWAY BUZZ 1988 PAPER 84 X 102 CM   2. SPIRITUAL HOME 1997 WOOD/RELIEF (DETAIL)   3. BLOW-UP 2000 PAPER 70 X 100 CM   4. ON VESEY STREET 2001 PAPER 21 X 25 CM   5. HOUSE AND GARDEN 1959 DRAWING

1

The curtain rises on a vast, primitive wasteland, not unlike certain parts of New Jersey …

Woody Allen

New York City 2003 – the bus to Newark Airport, operated by the proudly titled 'Olympia Trails Bus Company', crosses a vast industrial wasteland in New Jersey – elevated skyways, old railroads, buzzing pylons, iron bridges and polluted canals. A brooding, apocalyptic landscape, usually only glimpsed through the smeared windows of the bus. This terrain has always been my point of arrival and departure into America. A dramatic and exhilarating ride – with all the anticipation of big adventures to follow.

Now there is sadness, though. New York has changed. This journey is no longer familiar, but disorientating. My two landmarks, on the tip of the Manhattan skyline, once seen from every stage of the ride, are gone.

1. HISTORY OF AMERICA 2002 DIPTYCH CANVAS 152 X 244 CM

Following Alec Clifton-Taylor's advice of
'when visiting a town, always look up'
I make sure I look down and sideways as well;
I also like to peer with my camera into reflections
in puddles, shop windows, distorted mirrors
broken glass and car windscreens …

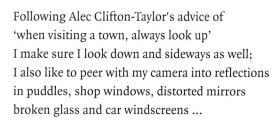

1. SLIPSTREAM 1993 PAPER 122 X 122 CM   2. FLUX 1999 PAPER 74 X 59 CM   3. NEW YORK WINDSCREENS 1999 PHOTOGRAPHS   4. LATE JUNCTION (BROADCASTING HOUSE, LONDON) 2002 PAPER 30 X 30 CM

Late Junction   Richard Hjelm. 02

... and at my feet the pale green Thames
lies like a rod of rippled jade

Oscar Wilde, from *Symphony in Yellow* 1881

1. CULTURE 1999 CANVAS 122 X 152 CM   2. (ANOTHER) WATERLOO SUNSET 1988 4 WORKS ON PAPER EACH 76 X 224 CM   3. GREEN RIVER 2003 CANVAS 60 X 60CM

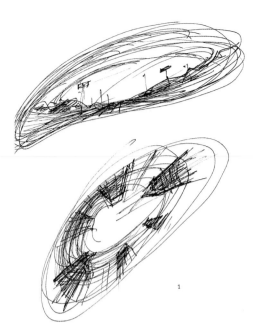

1. CITY SWIRLS 1996 SKETCHBOOK   2. SPINNING LONDON 1996 PAPER 70 X 100 CM

The City of London since the 1980s – an armada of cranes in a sea of construction. The shiny temples of fake marble and smoked glass built in the Thatcher era have been succeeded by the blob-like shapes of Norman Foster's 'Gherkin' and 'Testicle', that mix computer-aided design with drug culture. From the rooftops it all looks like Legoland ....

London has never been entirely at ease with its future.

1. DOODLEBUG (FESTIVAL HALL) 2000 CANVAS 31 X 31 CM   2. PINK ECONOMIST 2000 CANVAS 152 X 117 CM   3. TATE 1995 PAPER 122 X 152 CM   4. COMMERCE 1999 CANVAS 122 X 152 CM

Battersea Power Station, a dying mammal. A dark husk left on the shoreline. An ancient sunset reflected in broken glass. Monumental. A ghost palace. This abandoned building has appeared in my work for twenty years. Occasionally glimpsed, sometimes fragmented. It bridges the old world with the new city, and now sits, awaiting its fate, alongside the railway and river barges ....

1. MONUMENTAL 1997 PAPER 152 X 122 CM   2. MONOLITHIC 1997 PAPER 152 X 122 CM(DETAIL)

Eight miles high over America.
Clear air turbulence.
Smudged vapour trails.
A tiny speck in a lonely sky.
Only desert below:
A silent, slow-motion world.
Dust tracks and irrigation circles.
A rumble of distant thunder.
Next gas 50 miles.

Still two hours to landing.
Pull down the blind.

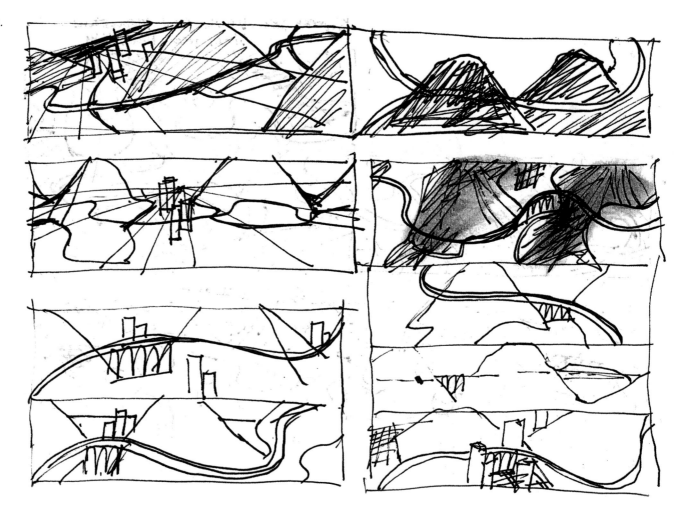

1. DESCENDING ANGELS 1990 PAPER 57 X 152 CM   2. LONG LANDSCAPES 1992 SKETCHBOOK

3. BIG SKY 1991 CANVAS 117 X 168 CM (DETAIL)

Los Angeles is the most beautiful and most ugly city in the world. Mountains, deserts and oceans surround a sprawling shanty town of billboards and neon. When you drive in from Palm Springs, a sign says 'Welcome to Los Angeles', but you still have over 100 miles to go. For me, all this adds to the visual appeal of the place: a fragile community perched on a fault line, superimposed on an infinite grid system stretching into the sunset ....

In Los Angeles ... finding the sneaky Schindler or the camouflaged Neutra ... that's the problem

Chris Dawson, *Gingerbread and Kitsch*, 1981

1. BEAUTIFUL INTERCHANGE 1988 PAPER 84 X 102 CM   2. SERIOUS SANTA MONICA SUNSET 1988 PAPER 84 X 102 CM   3. FREEWAY KARMA 1988 PAPER 84 X 102 CM

City of lost angels. Death, narcissism and fire. Health cults and criminal smog. Sick cops and saintly sinners. Beach and forest. Paradise and hell.

John Rechy, from The Sexual Outlaw 1977

1. NIGHT TRAIN 1988 PAPER 84 X 102 CM   2. THE WORLD AT ONE 1986 PAPER 76 X 56 CM   3. DOWNTOWNER 1986 PAPER 56 X 38 CM   4. ANDRE OF HOLLYWOOD 1986 PAPER 38 X 56 CM

Winter 1979 – I took the Greyhound
bus from New York to Los Angeles.
It being February, I took the
southerly route through Dallas.
As I was eating and sleeping on the
road for five days, I wore loose-
fitting army fatigues for comfort.
An elderly couple (who got on at
Mobile, Alabama, and got off, 48
hours later, at Quartzsite, Arizona)
were convinced I was a Vietnam Vet,
and treated me like a national hero,
despite the fact we had swapped life
stories. Perhaps they thought I was
hallucinating ....

The horizons opened out and the
skies got bigger – I saw this journey
as my rite of passage.

*You're on the old bus and the old bus
is on the old road*

Lewis Furey, from *Caught You* 1975

1. TRANCE AMERIKA 1996 PAPER 50 X 70 CM   2. AFTER THE HEAT 1986 PAPER 56 X 76 CM   3. UTAH 1988 PHOTOGRAPH   4. SPACE ADVENTURES 1996 PAPER 70 X 100 CM

1

1. SURF CITY (HERE WE COME), SANTA MONICA 1986 SUPER-8 STILLS

Berlin, Summer 1982 – the Ku-damm, Café Krantzler, the spinning Mercedes logo ... and glimpsed, at the ends of leafy, residential streets, the Wall – all pock-marked concrete and graffiti. The east, a forbidden horizon of grey blocks ... the west, muggy and airless and decadent .... Fifteen years later, the Potsdamer Platz, all shiny and corporate, was rising from the ashes.

A new plan, a new city, laid over an old map, an old world.

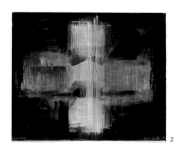

1. NEIGHBOURHOOD THREAT 1985 PAPER 76 X 56 CM   2. REICHSTAG 1995 PAPER 122 X 152 CM   3. METAMORPHOSIS 1998 PAPER 152 X 122 CM(DETAIL)   4. BERLIN 1982 SKETCHBOOK

Hamburg – a rich northern city. Big ships on the mighty Elbe. Woods and lakes and BMWs. I remember signing 2000 catalogues in 1992. No break, just champagne and laughter. Modern Hamburgers – art lovers and Anglophiles ....

1. SPRINKENHOF 1995 PAPER 153 X 122 CM   2. STADT 1999 CANVAS 142 X 124 CM   3. HAVEN 1999 CANVAS 108 X 153 CM   4. CHILEHAUS REVISITED 1996 PAPER 76 X 56 CM

December 2000 – a city of still, monochromatic reflections. Dark buildings set against skeletal trees and an opaque sky. I was interested in what the tourists never see, Stalinist palaces, proto-modernist villas, and concrete bunkers.

Bridge pos/neg.

Bata store

Underground Station.

Baba villas?

New Opera House

Holiday Inn
(Stalinist Wedding Cake
In The Suburbs)

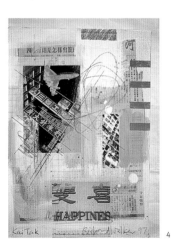

December 1991 – a commission in the Far East for shipping insurers. I stayed for a week in Singapore under leaden skies. It never stopped raining. In Hong Kong, I took a bus that snaked up a mountain to visit a giant, gold Buddha. In Bangkok, I hid from the noise and traffic fumes in temple courtyards and ate fresh pineapple.

I felt different here, but never really at home.

1. THE FUTURE NOW 1996 PAPER 152 X 122 CM   2. HONG KONG HIGH 1995 PAPER 85 X 104 CM   3. BRAVE NEW WORLD 1992 PAPER 100 X 70 CM   4. KAI TAK 1997 CANVAS 36 X 25 CM

japan between cultures
happy in a bigger ordeal
small clouds of otherness
such beauty in distress

1. OVER UTOPIA 1992 PAPER 70 X 100 CM   2. FLOATING TECHNOLOGY 1993 SKETCHBOOK   3. SINGAPORE 1992 TREATED POSTCARD   4. MATERIAL WORLD (BANGKOK) 1998 PAPER 100 X 70 CM (DETAIL)

Winter 1995 – once upon a time I wanted to be an architect. The careers master at school, whose office was an old tin hut down by the river, said I was no good at maths, so a job in architecture was out of the question. 'Had I thought about commercial art?' he suggested. 'What an idiot!' was my father's reaction, when I told him the tale.

Years later, I was invited to collaborate with a team of architects, based in London. We designed glass panels to be suspended at jaunty angles in an atrium. I had a desk and a phone, I attended meetings and I built a model, which looked really impressive. Project managers came and went, and eventually the scheme fell victim to 'health and safety' and fizzled out. I then returned to my old life of blissful solitude in my studio.

So I suppose I fulfilled my childhood dream, and I'm still no good at maths.

1. PROJECT FOR BT, LONDON 1995 MODEL (NIGHT)   2. PROJECT FOR BT, LONDON 1995 MODEL (DAY)   3. FROZEN MUSIC 2001 CANVAS 92 X 92 CM

I have a little fantasy, that half an hour before they let the general public into National Trust properties the volunteers (usually no-nonsense ladies of a certain age) march around the corridors chanting in unison 'lovely old, nasty new, lovely old, nasty new'.

1. ANCIENT MODERN 2001 CANVAS 92 X 92 CM   2. SCRATCH TV 1994 MONOPRINT 49 X 49 CM   3. FUTURE SHAPE OF LONDON 1996 PAPER 35 X 50 CM   4. NO. 2, WILLOW ROAD 1996 PAPER 35 X 50 CM

brilliant living
with big forms
there's head space
inside my blue decay
smudge of grey
I dream of white heat
clear glass
sharp horizon

pure
outside my clutter

4

1

2

3

5

1. ARCHITECT'S EYE 1995 PAPER 70 X100 CM   2. OUTSIDE IN 1994 PAPER/RELIEF 49 X 49 CM   3. BRAVE BLUE WORLD 1994 PAPER/RELIEF 49 X 49 CM
4. DREAM TECHNOLOGY 1995 PAPER 70 X 100 CM   5. SUPERSTRUCTURE 1999 PAPER 128 X 102CM

The physician can bury his mistakes, but the architect can only advise his client to plant vines

Frank Lloyd Wright

In the 1960s, I used to walk my dog across building sites near my home. They were constructing Span houses amongst the cedar trees and rhododendrons. These were exciting and modern, inspired by Scandinavian design and aimed at the new Habitat generation.

In 2004, I rekindled my enthusiasm by leading an architectual tour around these (now iconic) housing estates.

1. INNER LANGUAGE 1997 WOOD/RELIEF   2. DREAMHOME 1996 PAPER 35 X 50 CM   3. CALIFORNIA NOCTURNE 1996 PAPER 50 X 70 CM

4. LE CORBUSIER IN INDIA 1996 50 X 70 CM   5. DESIGN FOR LIVING (SPAN) 1994 SKETCHBOOK   6. WRIGHT -SITE 1997 WOOD/RELIEF

Talking about music is like dancing about architecture

Elvis Costello

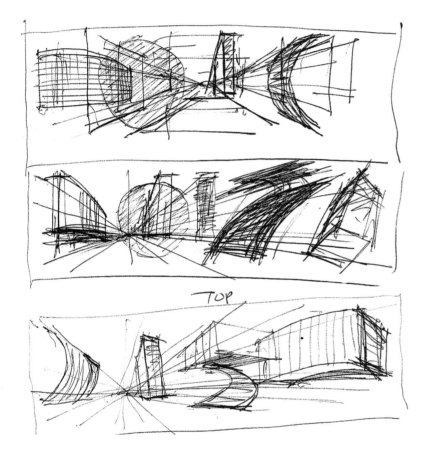

*... my first sketches are the clue to everything that follows.
For when the first idea is deep enough, life is too short to
expound it fully ...*

Erich Mendelsohn 1930s

1. DANCING ARCHITECTURE 1999 SKETCHBOOK   2. SPACE JAZZ NO. 3 1992 PAPER 81 X 149 CM

3. DYNAMICS 1999 PAPER 74 X 59 CM (DETAIL)

I've always loved the smell of screenprinting ink and all the activity in a printmaking studio. I always get a thrill from seeing an image appearing, from underneath a screen, for the very first time. I'm still inspired by the element of surprise and the endless possibilities of multiples and variations. I remember, back at Camberwell, there was a hard core of screenprinters. We all used to work late, then end up in the bar – usually completely high from a day breathing in chemicals ….

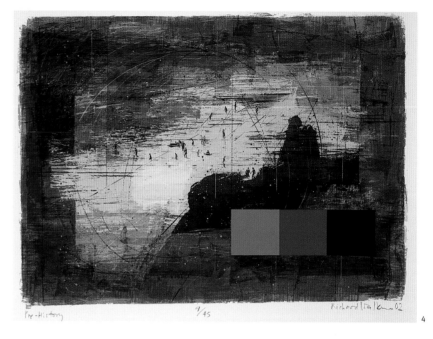

1. RUN 2000 SCREENPRINT 42 X 35 CM   2. HIT 2000 SCREENPRINT 42 X 35 CM   3. RISE 2000 SCREENPRINT 42 X 35 CM   4. PRE-HISTORY 2002 SCREENPRINT 72 X 90 CM   5. CLOUD DIARY 2002 SCREENPRINT 72 X 90 CM

Whatever you can do, or dream you can, begin it. Boldness has genius, power and magic in it

Goethe

1. SAN GIMIGNANO 2003 PHOTOGRAPHS

1

Romanticism is precisely situated neither in choice of subject, nor in exact truth, but in a mode of feeling

Baudelaire

2

3

4

5

1. BLACK SUN 2003 PAPER 21 X 25 CM   2. RED EARTH 2003 PAPER 21 X 25 CM   3. EAST EDGE 2003 PAPER 21 X 25 CM   4. X-MOON 2003 PAPER 21 X 25 CM   5. HUNGRY OCEAN GAIN 2003 CANVAS 183 X 183 CM

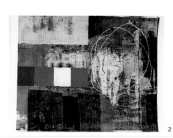

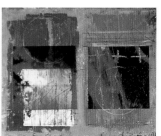

Whether it is possible to 'go modern' and still 'be British' is a question vexing quite a few people today ....

Paul Nash, *Weekend Review* London 1932

1. FALSE HEART'S HISTORY 2003 CANVAS 183 X 183 CM 2. OLD SCHOOL 2001 PAPER 21 X 25 CM 3. FILM STUDIES 2001 PAPER 21 X 25 CM 4. PALMER'S MOON 2001 PAPER 21 X 25 CM 5. FOR KENNETH ANGER 2001 PAPER 21 X 25CM

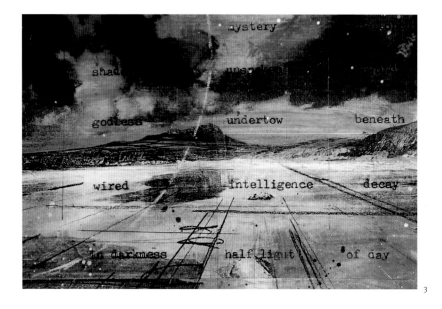

Dungeness has luminous skies: its moods can change like quicksilver. A small cloud has the effect of a thunderstorm in the city; the days have a drama I could never conjure up on an opera stage.

Derek Jarman, from *Modern Nature* 1989

1. ENGLAND MADE ME 2001 PAPER 21 X 25 CM 2. X-DREAMS 2001 PAPER 21 X 25 CM 3. UNSPOKEN 2002 CANVAS 60 X 60 CM(DETAIL) 4. MOON 2003 CANVAS 20 X 20 CM(DETAIL) 5. DAYS OF ECHO 2004 CANVAS 183 X 183 CM

A CONVERSATION

Richard Walker (RW) and Peter Parker (PP)

PP: You've always used sketchbooks, haven't you?

RW: Yes, my ideas were just put down as drawings and I suppose they came together as books. I always had drawing books as a child.

PP: At school we all had something called a 'doodle book', didn't we?

RW: That's right, but I think I took doodle books on to another plane, because no one illustrated them, they just did so-called creative writing in them or wrote poems. I turned them into lavishly illustrated productions. There was a burgeoning book-design idea going on there. I always follow things through, and I can relate to what I was doing then even now. I can see the beginnings in the drawing books I did as a child right through the school books to college where I started to keep sketchbooks – and of course I've kept all my sketchbooks since then. They're very important to me because they're my archive. I think for anybody – a painter or a writer – it's very important to have an archive so you can see the workings, revisit your own past, see how you actually thought about something twenty years ago, which I find fascinating.

PP: Robin Noscoe was a big influence, wasn't he?

RW: Yes. When we were at school I thought everyone had an inspiring art teacher. Later on I realised that a lot of people didn't in fact have a very interesting art education. I was very fortunate with Robin. Not only was he an influence on my work, but also on my taste and style. You weren't really aware of it, he just set things up around you and let things happen. You didn't really think you were being taught, you didn't know till later that you'd actually learned a lot. He saw no value in academic exams – actually, when I did my history of art 'A' Level he left all the books out on the table!

I kept up with Robin after leaving school and although he was getting older he was involved with new ideas in his work and we became sounding-boards for each other. He never thought that he knew more than you.

LIFE DRAWING 2000

PORKY'S CLAM BAR
SKETCHBOOK 1981

Bayshore, Long Island, N.Y.
July '81

PP: Music's always been very important in your thinking.

RW: Yes, there's always been a soundtrack going on in the background when I'm working. I pick up lyrics, I pick up titles, I pick up the moods of music of the period and they've always entered into my work in some way.

PP: In the work you did after you'd been through art school, you used pop-music iconography, pop stars and celebrities.

RW: That was my theme at art school, really, which is interesting because if you look at a lot of artists' work now they've come back to that. I suppose that I was using, for want of a better word, 'trashy' subject-matter inspired by people like Rauschenberg, who used everyday imagery, and of course Warhol, who was using pop iconography. I was working in the 1970s, but I was carrying on that 1960s tradition.

PP: Well, you certainly got very early into the cult of celebrity,

but you were always very satirical about it. You even invented alternative personae for yourself.

RW: Yes, there was Kiss Laminated, a narcissistic New York socialite. That name I found on some instructions for packing sheets of plastic.

PP: And Gabriel Blade, a ghastly poseur whose name was derived from Gay Young Blade.

RW: When I think about it, a lot of these characters came out of the kitchen drawer! There were these cooking utensils with names like Reposo Shred and Mouli Parsmint.

PP: I seem to remember that a Reposo Shred was some sort of grater and a Mouli Parsmint was a tool for chopping herbs.

RW: Yes, then there was a make of cooker, a Tricity Viscount. I adopted that name for a middle-aged woman who painted flowers and landscapes, and I actually did some paintings under her name to see if they would sell. I'm pleased to say they didn't.

PP: Many of your pictures could be described as portraits of buildings. Where did this interest in architecture come from?

RW: From an early age I wanted to be an architect and I was always drawing house plans. Then, when I went to New York, I saw for the first time these monumental buildings which you couldn't ignore. The word 'portrait' is apt because they had real presence and character. Later I became more interested in the space and the light than in the buildings themselves, and the pictures became more abstract. I see myself at that point between abstraction and figuration, and architecture gave me some sort of structure which I could use in my work without being too specific about it.

PP: You don't believe in pure abstraction?

RW: Personally, I think you have to abstract from a subject.

I'm always interested in seeing the early work of abstract painters and often find that it is figurative – and that pleases me because I then know where it originated. I don't think abstraction can come out of thin air.

PP: Words have played an important part in your work. Your titles are always very carefully chosen, but you have also incorporated texts into the actual paintings.

RW: That goes back to school again. Of course we were very keen on poetry in those days. In the 1960s the whole concept of concrete poetry was about imagery rather than making sense, which I thought was interesting but never really taken far enough. I always thought that words and images should go together – and indeed sounds should also be part of it, so that it should be a complete experience. I've always loved wordplay, which may have something to do with the fact that my grandfather used to compile crossword puzzles!

PP: You also use a lot of quotations, don't you?

RW: Yes. As titles for more recent paintings I've used words from Shakespeare's sonnets, which when divorced from their original meaning form rather beautiful phrases. Just isolated words put together, as in 'Hungry Ocean Gain' or 'False Heart's History'.

PP: Yes, seeing those titles you wouldn't immediately think of the *Sonnets* or even of Shakespeare.

RW: Yes, I want them to take on a life of their own, but also retain their original resonance.

PP: Do you have the titles of paintings in your head as you work or do they come afterwards? I saw in your sketchbooks that there were long lists of titles.

RW: Yes, they're queuing up! Sometimes I do a painting and then look down a list to see which title fits it, or *vice versa*. I would never call something 'Untitled # 10' or 'Composition # 3'.

PP: And what about the title of this book?

RW: Well, it's partly a pun. 'Image and Myth' goes back to the 1970s, when I first showed my work at Minsky's Gallery in London. We were always making up characters, and one of them was Imogen Myth, the art critic. But apart from that, it's a succinct phrase that describes what my work is all about.

PP: In a lot of your work the central images have been taken from photographs, but now you're going back into art history and using paintings. Is this a new direction for you?

RW: Ten years ago I did a series of paintings of British architecture built in my lifetime in which I made stylistic references to English artists such as Hitchens, Hodgkin, Nicholson and Piper. As you grow older, you have your own history that you can use and I've now gone back further, to the paintings I studied at school.

PP: Would you say that you have deconstructed these old paintings?

RW: Yes. For example I've recently used Böcklin's *Island of the Dead*, which is certainly an interesting and mysterious picture. I've experimented with the composition, juxtaposing it with elements of modern architecture, bringing together the past and the present.

PP: Sometimes in your sketchbooks an idea is worked up elaborately and then, a few pages on, it's worked down again.

RW: That's the beauty of a sketchbook: you can see the workings, the way I'm thinking. And sometimes I need to know the way I'm thinking. Sometimes you look back at your old work not just for inspiration but to see how you were thinking at a certain point in time. I do think in layers and a lot of my work is often built up in layers – layers of ideas, layers of textures, layers of thinking.

ILLUMINATED MAN
SKETCHBOOK 1985

PP: Is there a danger that you can over-think your work?

RW: I know I have a tendency to do this, because I have a great attention to detail in everything I do, so I just have to put something down or turn it away from me so I don't overwork it. And often I start to reduce a painting when I'm half-way through because I realise it's getting too busy and over-complicated. I start to strip it back.

PP: People who know your work for its urban images may be surprised to see an English ruralist theme in your most recent paintings.

RW: I think I'd investigated the architectural elements to the point where they became invisible, but the structure and the space were still there. I suddenly became aware, by looking at the work of other artists, that I had neglected the English countryside.

PP: Just as your earlier pictures were about the 'idea' of New York, so your new work is about an 'idea' of England. And 'England' in the popular imagination is the countryside.

RW: Yes, absolutely – and that's where the myth comes in.

PP: It seems to me that the basic difference is that the pictures of New York were celebratory, whereas the pictures of the English countryside are elegiac. The skyscrapers were triumphant in your work, but the countryside seems threatened, perhaps passing into history. I wonder if this is related to your interest in the English folk-music tradition that goes back to your schooldays?

RW: Yes, I think my New York pictures were a celebration of the exterior, but these new pictures are certainly a journey into the interior. I now feel that by opening out my subject-matter I can embrace ideas that fell by the wayside earlier on.

PP: I'd like to ask you about the scale of your works, which varies from large canvases to small works on paper. Do you feel that some subjects demand larger physical dimensions than others?

RW: I like the contrast between vast paintings, which are related to the murals I've done, and the small paintings, which are jewel-like and more personal.

PP: You also produce diptychs or triptychs or paintings that belong in groups.

RW: That also comes from my public projects and a realisation that my work can be exhibited as an installation. You set out a coherent series of images in a gallery rather than just a collection of individual paintings.

PP: That reminds me of your degree show, which was mounted like a stage-set. It wasn't just pictures hung on the wall, it was a designed space.

RW: Yes, I was trying to get away from doing things in a conventional way. I had drawings, screenprints, photographs and newspaper cuttings – and I wondered how I was going to display all this material. My solution was to hang them on several overlapping washing-lines, using lighting to create the illusion of a stage-set.

PP: And are your public projects usually related to the paintings you're doing at the time?

RW: Yes – in particular the windows I did for Barney's in New York, where I wanted to create the illusion of a large architectural space. I did drawings on transparent perspex panels which I then suspended in front of mannequins.

PP: In fact, very like when you use a photographic image and then draw over it.

RW: That's right: it was a three-dimensional version of something I might do in my sketchbook.

PP: So it's always back to the sketchbook?

RW: Absolutely.

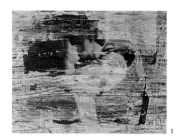

The Dream Reel series was a loosely linked group of small canvases, which were a mixture of sparse, textured landscapes, fleeting moments from classical mythology, grainy cinema stills and the flickering static from TV screens. They suggested a contact sheet of photographs or the shifting locations of a bank of security cameras.

Here, I developed a 'painterly' technique of merging photo-imagery with prepared artwork, spontaneously 'within the camera', involving multiple exposures, blurred imagery and random settings. The finished pieces were then enlarged, re-worked and mounted on to canvas.

... dreaming is nursed in darkness ... Jean Genet

1. SECRET 2003 CANVAS 23 X 30.5 CM 2. MOVIE 2003 CANVAS 23 X 30.5 CM 3. PIAZZA 2003 CANVAS 23 X 30.5 CM 4. INSECTS 2003 CANVAS 23 X 30.5 CM 5. ECHO 2003 CANVAS 23 X 30.5 CM

As a child, I had a copy of *Peacock Pie* by Walter de la Mare. This was a collection of melancholic verse about sick children and consumptive adults. I remember being haunted by Edward Ardizzone's scratchy illustrations.

This 'otherness' continued into the stories of Rupert Bear, where animals in Edwardian costumes appeared in lush landscapes and girl guides skipped through sinister woods.

Later on, during my teenage years, I was fascinated by nineteenth-century paintings – the image of Ophelia floating downstream on a river of flowers, the body of Chatterton stretched out in an attic bedroom, and the brooding symbolist landscapes of Caspar David Friedrich.

Then there were the darker Beatle songs, dealing with loneliness and depression, like 'Eleanor Rigby' and 'I'm So Tired'. David Bowie sang about his brother's insanity in 'All the Madmen', Andy Warhol revealed, in his Factory movies, a tragic humour on the streets of New York City, and, later, Gilbert and George celebrated in their art their curious and austere existence together in London's East End.

There were also films such as *Peeping Tom*, *Rosemary's Baby*, *Blue Velvet* and *Eraserhead* that inhabited their own space and revealed a parallel world of 'otherness'.

It is the notion of this parallel world that interests me. Something not far below the surface. Something not mentioned. Something of the night ....

Several years ago, when faced with the choice of seeing either *Sensation* at London's Royal Academy, or the little exhibition in the Sackler Gallery upstairs, I picked the latter: *Victorian Fairy Painting* was far stranger and more radical than anything on show downstairs, going under the label 'cutting-edge'.

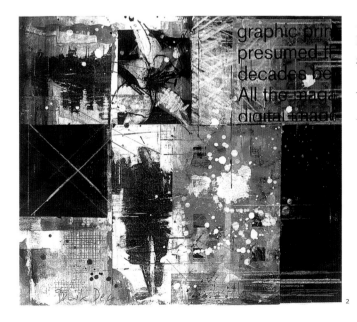

... and never from her window looked out Mrs Gill on the Fairy shrilly mocking in the garden

Walter de la Mare, from *The Mocking Fairy* 1913

1. SUPER-8 2002 PAPER 25 X 21 CM   2. DARK DECADE 2001 PAPER 21 X 25 CM

Beech leaves, that yellow the noon-time,
Float past like specks in the eye;
I set every tree in my June time,
And now they obscure the sky

Thomas Hardy, from
At Day-close in November 1909

Soldiers and sailors have just come from war,
been fighting for their Queen and country, 'tis sure.
Come home to be starved, better stayed where they were,
and it's, oh, the hard times of old England.

English folk song, the Copper Family, 1955

1. CONVERSATIONS WITH TREES 2004 PHOTOGRAPHS   2. ODYSSEY 2004 CANVAS 23 X 30.5 CM   3. MAP OF DREAMS 2004 PAPER 30 X 30 CM(DETAIL)   4. HARD TIMES OF OLD ENGLAND 2003 CANVAS 183 X 183CM

searching
for an identical mind
shooting
in a random nature
hunting
for the real thing
in the middle
of a lost idea

the america I know
has few clues
the sightings of god
do not fit the pattern

It is the awful void that hits you when you look south, and you
are convinced the Twin Towers are just kneeling down out of sight
to fool you, either that or you keep hoping they will pop up in a
cornfield in Iowa – I fear sadly they will not ...

Virginia Buchan, Chinatown, New York, 2001

1. BLACK WATCH 2004 CANVAS 60 X 60 CM(DETAIL)   2. BLUE MANHATTAN 2001 PHOTOGRAPH   3. LIFE DURING WARTIME 2001 CANVAS 61 X 61 CM

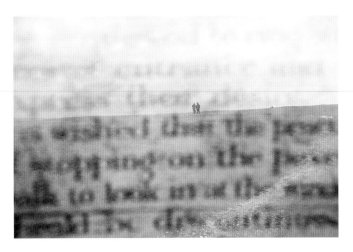
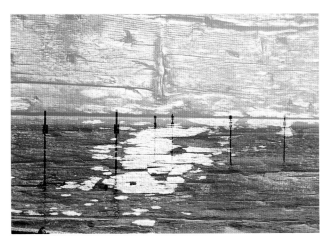

*We could hear it
before the shutters were open
the wind on the beach …
no one walking
not even the dogs.
A day
for the rubbish to dance*

Alfreda Benge, from *Sight of the Wind* 1991

1. ENGLISH HORIZONS 2003 PHOTOGRAPHS

When I hear cathedral music, I really don't so much
listen to the music as listen to the building

John Cale 2004

I have always listened to music while I am working. I
remember as a child lying on the floor with my drawing book
hearing the muffled sounds of Beatles records coming from
my sister's bedroom. At school, there was always a Radio 3
concert on in the mornings in the art studios.

Now, I find myself selecting music for a certain mood and
activity – something fast and rhythmic for the physical act of
pouring paint on to a canvas; something soft and sensual for
finer detail and mixing colours.

Certain seasons and conditions suggest certain music. I often
play Terry Riley's 'A Rainbow in Curved Air' on a bright,
optimistic summer morning. Shirley and Dolly Collins's
'Anthems in Eden' is played on 1st May, whatever the weather.
Brian Eno's installation pieces are useful to create a warm
atmosphere, but with just a touch of menace.

Sometimes, I have a break and turn on the radio. In many of
my works produced since 11 September 2001, there have been
'interruptions', where my mood has been changed by some
grave world event or disaster heard on the news, and then
these thoughts weave their way into a current painting.

Quite often, I can get so involved in what I am doing that I
leave the radio on all day, which can expose me
to all sorts of floating anxieties and random emotions; which,
in turn, can lead to all sorts of interesting possibilities ....

Since the early 1990s I have made my own music, making
tapes using keyboard, sampler and, often, found objects. I
now have a large archive, which I play either in the studio or
at exhibitions. I like to see it as the aural companion to my
visual work.

London 1984 – one winter's day, I went out and bought a Super-8 camera, a projector and a splicer. Inspired by the grainy quality and radical beauty of certain low-budget underground movies, such as Kenneth Anger's *Scorpio Rising*, Andy Warhol's *Chelsea Girls*, Peter Greenaway's *Vertical Features Remake* and Derek Jarman's *Angelic Conversation*, I launched into 'film diary' mode, and made a series of little movies about anything and everything. At the same time, I had been invited to work with a company making pop videos and TV commercials. All this was new to me, and most of the time, I didn't have a clue what I was doing, so I just experimented and hoped for the best.

Luckily, I did somehow manage to produce a video for Stephen Duffy's song 'Kiss Me', which won an industry award for best art direction.

Making a movie is casting a spell

Kenneth Anger

1. FLIP, BLIP, DIP 2004 TRIPTYCH CANVAS 10 X 30 CM   2. PLANE 1985 SUPER-8 STILL   3. FRUIT 1985 SUPER-8 STILL

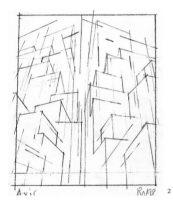

Murals, Axis restaurant, One Aldwych, London – a review

The canopy of a stylized forest of skyscrapers explodes towards the viewer, an accelerated metropolis seen through the ultimate fish-eye lens; standing in the mezzanine bar overlooking the restaurant at Axis, one immediately feels an urge to grab the nearest solid object to calm the vertigo induced by Richard Walker's remarkable mural.

The bar becomes the gondola of a pre-war Zeppelin, cruising airily over a city of the future – and this is wholly appropriate, for Walker's dynamic imagery, quivering with momentum and straining to break free from its surroundings, immediately recalls the Futurists, who felt so connected to the kinetics of the new technology of flight that their art took on its form as a dizzying, kaleidoscopic whirl of colour and shape, urgent with the future and all it contained. Indeed, one can easily imagine Tullio Crali's Before the Parachute opens transplanted to the roof of one of Walker's thrusting structures, though so vertiginous are they that even Crali's enthusiastic sampler of the air might have delayed his departure from terra firma here.

From the restaurant, the mural is even more arresting. Like eyes in the best portraits, the probing finger-like forms of the towers seem to follow the viewer around the room, evidence of an intelligent response on Walker's part to the gently concave form of the walls. Here, too, one appreciates his use of flat planes of colour to delineate the buildings simply but powerfully, placing the piece firmly in the tradition of Demuth and Sheeler, artists from the New World whose concern with technology, modernity and the new urban landscape used similar means of expression.

Finally, tucked under the spiral stair linking bar and restaurant, a smaller strip mural shows what is effectively a reverse view of the same fabulous city, towers this time rising from a neon evening streetscape and disappearing into the sky. The angle is much lower, more reassuringly familiar, and is that available from a car, that other manifestation of speed and futurity that was so celebrated between the wars.

As diners relax in this intimate space, do they try to picture the residents of this magical city that Walker has created? Might Tamara de Lempicka's angular Modernes relax on their sofas behind the skyscrapers' glass, or drive their sports cars along the hidden roads? One must surely hope so.

Chris Rogers

1. CLUSTER 1998 PAPER 62 X 46 CM   2. AXIS 1998 LINE DRAWING   3. AXIS (RED) 1998 SKETCH   4. AXIS RESTAURANT MURAL NO. 2 1998   5. AXIS (OCHRE) 1998 SKETCH   6. AXIS RESTAURANT (MAIN MURAL) 1998

Autumn 2000 – Simon Doonan, Manhattan's own fashion guru, asked me to create three window displays for Barney's, the exclusive store on Madison Avenue. Simon, over the years, has caused sensation and brought traffic to a standstill with his outrageous and controversial windows, so I jumped at the offer. In my studio, I started making little models with cut-out figures, which I lit and photographed. The resulting images looked more like designs for modern dance or sets for musicals than window displays. Everything was moving. Simon said I'd have a problem twisting his mannequins into the positions I wanted, so I'd have to compromise. When I arrived in New York to start work, fate had already intervened. I had just broken three ribs back in England, and I was in a lot of pain, so there was little chance of producing anything with much movement. I suppose I could have sat in the sidelines, shouting out instructions and pointing with a stick, but it wouldn't have been the same. With a combination of sheer determination and strong painkillers, I didn't do such a bad job in the end, but there wasn't any dancing ....

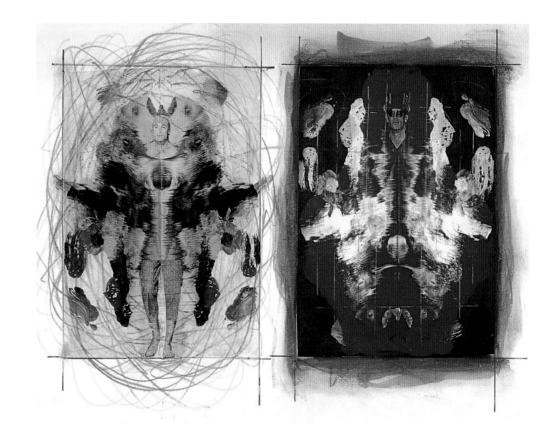

I never think that people die. They just go to department stores Andy Warhol

1. BARNEYS (RED WINDOW) 2000   2. BARNEYS (BLUE WINDOW) 2000   3. AND 4. BARNEYS WINDOWS 2000 MODEL (2 VARIATIONS)   5. DESIGNS FOR BARNEYS 2000 SKETCHBOOK

The Wall of Glass stretches the entire length of a new nightclub in the Hyatt Hotel in Warsaw. Images were digitally printed onto glass panels, which, when assembled, overlapped each other, creating a rhythmical series of planes. This was then lit from above and below, focusing on the interesting visual patterns and combinations that occured accidently as it was put together – something that usually goes unnoticed on paper or at the design stage.

5

1. GLASS WALL, HYATT HOTEL, WARSAW 2002   2. GLASS WALL (INSTALLATION DAY) 2002

Projects, such as the cow for the London Cow Parade 2002, the mask for the Prince's Trust in 1996, Barney's windows, the Wall of Glass, and the Axis mural are all part of a whole – so long as I can experiment within a framework, have the challenge of working in different scales, and am able to use new materials and techniques ... I am happy.

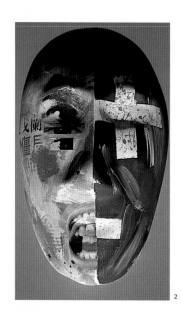

Formula of my happiness: a Yes, a No, a straight line, a goal ...

Friedrich Nietzsche, from *Twilight of the Idols* 1889

1. LITTLE ANGEL 1997 WOOD   2. MASK FOR THE PRINCE'S TRUST 1996   3. ANGEL/DREAM 1997 WOOD SCREEN (DETAIL)
4. BATTERSEA COW POWER (LONDON COW PARADE) 2002   5. ANGELIC CONVERSATION 1996 PAPER 70 X 100 CM

1. UN-EARTH 2002 CANVAS 152 X 122 CM(DETAIL)

1954   Born Yorkshire, England
1967–71 Canford School, Dorset
1972   Kingston School of Art, Surrey (Foundation)
1973   Camberwell School of Art, London (BA Graphic Arts)
1976   Chelsea School of Art, London (MA Printmaking)

SOLO EXHIBITIONS
1978   One-Man Show Business, Minsky's Gallery, London
1979   Twilight Zones, Thumb Gallery, London
1980   RW3/NW1, Minsky's Gallery, London
1981   Uneasy Living, Thumb Gallery, London
1982   Bodily Fictions, Minsky's Gallery, London
1982   Body /Building, April Bar, Amsterdam
1983   Secret Surfaces, Centre 181, Hammersmith, London
1985   Illuminations, Minsky's Gallery, London
1986   The World at One, Thumb Gallery, London
1987   Inbetweentimes, Minsky's Gallery, London
1988   Street Language, Thumb Gallery, London
1988   Speed of Life, Madison Galleries, Los Angeles
1989   Working Titles, Minsky's Gallery, London
1990   Urban Nature, Thumb Gallery, London
1992   Exploded Views 1, Poster-Galerie, Hamburg
1992   Exploded Views 2, Hilo Pictures, Bonn
1993   Exploded Views 3, Galerie 2000, Berlin
1993   City Sensations, Jill George Gallery, London
1994   Modern Movements, Jill George Gallery, London
1996   International Language, Galerie Meissner/Glaxo-Wellcome, Hamburg
1996   Global Visions, New Academy Gallery, London
1997   In the Mix, New Academy Gallery, London
1998   Metropolitan, New Academy Gallery, London
1998   Metro/Mix, Lawrence Graham, London
1999   Motion Pictures, University of Brighton
1999   United Shapes, Galerie Meissner, Hamburg
2000   Infrastructure, New Academy Gallery, London
2000   Revisited, Canford School, Dorset
2000   City:Sites, Curwen Gallery, London
2001   Punk/Pastoral. White Gallery, Brighton
2002   World's Edge, New Academy Gallery, London
2003   A Dream Reel, Zimmer Stewart Gallery, Arundel, Sussex
2004   Days of Echo, Curwen Gallery, London
2004   Edge of England, Zimmer Stewart Gallery, Arundel, Sussex
2004   Image and Myth, Curwen Gallery, London

GROUP EXHIBITIONS
Since 1977 regular gallery shows at:
Minsky's Gallery, Thumb Gallery, Jill George Gallery,
New Academy Gallery, Curwen Gallery, London
Madison Galleries, Los Angeles, Galerie Meissner, Hamburg,
White Gallery, Brighton; also –

Surface Tension, Flavio Belli Gallery, Toronto;
Urban Landscapes,British Council Touring Exhibition;
Three Decades of ILEA Art Schools, Royal Academy,London;London Tourist Board,
Smiths Gallery, London;
A Decade of Printmaking, Camberwell Collage of Art, London;
Paintings Of Modern Life, Guildford House Gallery;
Prague, New Academy Gallery, London.
Art Fairs include: Printmaking at the Barbican Gallery, London;
Paintings at Bath, Los Angeles, London (ART 1998, 1999, 2002)
and Art Fair Cologne 2001. Discerning Eye 2003, London

PROJECTS / INSTALLATIONS
1985   Art Direction (Animation, Film and Video) ,
        Big Features, London
1991   Travel Commission - Sinclair, Roche and Temperly
        (Hong Kong and Singapore)
1995   Suspended Glass Project with British Telecom
        and RMJM Architects, London
1996   Masks Project, Prince's Trust, Royal Festival Hall, London
1998   Mural at Axis Restaurant, One Aldwych Hotel, London
2000   Three Window Installations, Barneys, New York
2002   Glass Wall Installation, Hyatt Hotel, Warsaw
2002   Cow Parade, London

PUBLIC / PRIVATE COLLECTIONS
Bankgesellschaft (London), BBC (Director General), Binder Hamlyn,
The British Council, BP Amoco, Channel Four Television,
Citicorp Intrenational Bank, Cleveland City Art Gallery, The Crown Estate,
Cruasid, Customs and Excise, De La Rue, Der Spiegel,
Excelsior Hotel – Heathrow, Fitch and Company, French Thornton,
Gurlings (London), Glaxo-Wellcome (Hamburg and Stevenage),
Hamburg Airport, Hamburg Sparkasse Bank,
Hammersmith and Fulham Council, London Electricity plc,
The London Lighthouse, London Tourist Board, Minerva Properties,
The National Theatre, London, RCA Corporation,
University of London (Queen Mary and Westfield College),
Sheffield City Art Gallery, Trowers Hamlyn, Vereins-West Bank,
Virgin Atlantic, World Travel Market, Westinghouse Corporation USA.

PUBLICATIONS
Artizan Editions (Limited Edition Screenprints)
King and McGaw (Posters)
Universal Prints, Hamburg (Posters)

LECTURING
1976 onwards   Lecturing in BA and MA Printmaking, Camberwell School of Art,
London. Also teaching at Kingston University, Brighton University and
Heatherleys School of Art.